JE Sterling   3/22

Where Does It Go?

Where Does Water Go?

by Charlie W. Sterling

Bullfrog
Books

Ideas for Parents and Teachers

Bullfrog Books let children practice reading informational text at the earliest reading levels. Repetition, familiar words, and photo labels support early readers.

Before Reading

- Discuss the cover photo. What does it tell them?

- Look at the picture glossary together. Read and discuss the words.

Read the Book

- "Walk" through the book and look at the photos. Let the child ask questions. Point out the photo labels.

- Read the book to the child, or have him or her read independently.

After Reading

- Prompt the child to think more. Ask: Have you thought about where water goes? What more do you want to learn about it?

Bullfrog Books are published by Jump!
5357 Penn Avenue South
Minneapolis, MN 55419
www.jumplibrary.com

Copyright © 2021 Jump! International copyright reserved in all countries. No part of this book may be reproduced in any form without written permission from the publisher.

Library of Congress Cataloging-in-Publication Data

Names: Sterling, Charlie W., author.
Title: Where does water go? / by Charlie W. Sterling.
Description: Minneapolis, MN : Jump!, [2021]
Bullfrog books | Includes index. | Audience: Ages 5–8.
Identifiers: LCCN 2020005961 (print)
LCCN 2020005962 (ebook)
ISBN 9781645275565 (hardcover)
ISBN 9781645275572 (paperback)
ISBN 9781645275589 (ebook)
Subjects: LCSH: Sewage disposal—Juvenile literature.
Classification: LCC TD741 .S74 2021 (print)
LCC TD741 (ebook) | DDC 628.3/6—dc23
LC record available at https://lccn.loc.gov/2020005961
LC ebook record available at https://lccn.loc.gov/2020005962

Editor: Jenna Gleisner
Designer: Molly Ballanger

Photo Credits: DamianPalus/iStock, cover; AlexussK/Shutterstock, 1; stuar/Shutterstock, 3; son Photo/Shutterstock, 4; Khosro/Shutterstock, 5; Dmitry Naumov/Shutterstock, 6–7, 22tl, 23tl; baona/iStock, 8, 22tr, 23tm; Love the wind/Shutterstock, 9; Lisaish/Shutterstock, 10–11; Vladimir Zapletin/iStock, 12–13, 22br, 23bl; savanterpor/Shutterstock, 14, 23tr; Bim/iStock, 15, 22bm; marekuliasz/Shutterstock, 16–17, 22bl, 23br; twohumans/iStock, 18–19 (top); Kdonmuang/Shutterstock, 18–19 (bottom), 23bm; Kdonmuang/Shutterstock, 20–21; Novac Vitali/Shutterstock, 24.

Printed in the United States of America at Corporate Graphics in North Mankato, Minnesota.

Table of Contents

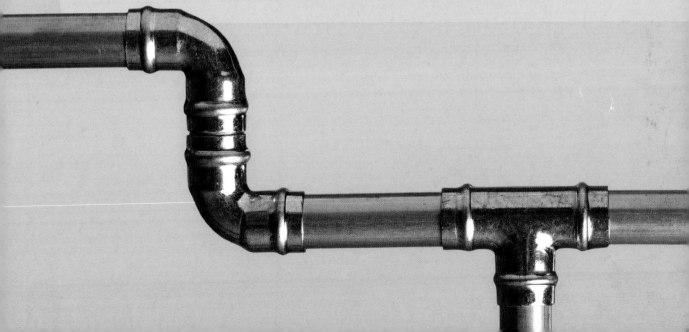

Down the Pipes

Dan flushes the toilet.

Bree washes her hands.

Water goes down the drain.
Then where does it go?

drain

Drains are connected to pipes.

pipe

Pipes carry water down.
Cool!

9

house
water
pipe

public
sewer
pipe

They connect to bigger pipes.

We can't see them.

Why?

They are under the ground.

They lead to the sewer.

sewer
tunnel

13

Then where?
The water goes to a plant.

wastewater treatment plant

It is cleaned.

water

It goes back into the water supply.

Like rivers!

Neat!

river

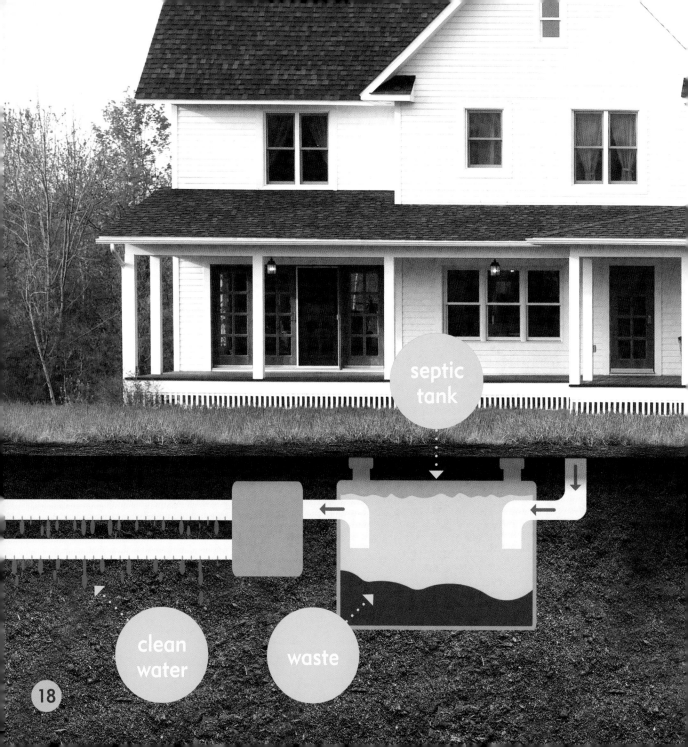

septic
tank

clean
water

waste

18

Some homes
have a tank.

It is under
the ground.

Water is cleaned.

It goes back into
the ground.

We use water every day.

Where does your water go?

Where Water Goes

What happens to water after it leaves your home if you don't have a septic tank? Take a look!

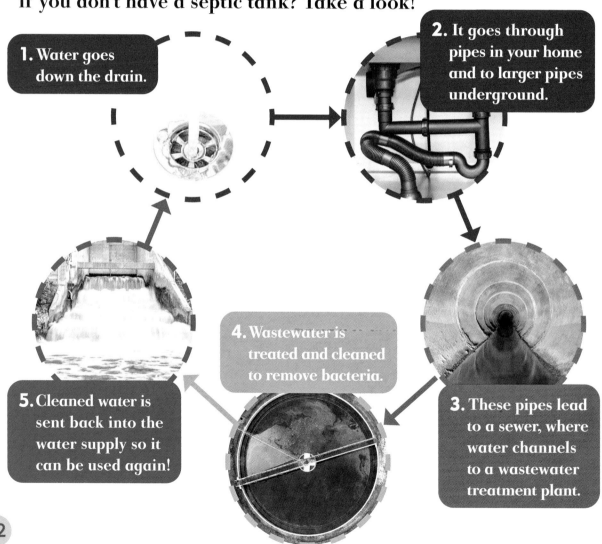

1. Water goes down the drain.

2. It goes through pipes in your home and to larger pipes underground.

3. These pipes lead to a sewer, where water channels to a wastewater treatment plant.

4. Wastewater is treated and cleaned to remove bacteria.

5. Cleaned water is sent back into the water supply so it can be used again!

Picture Glossary

drain
An opening leading to a pipe that takes away liquid.

pipes
Tubes that carry liquids or gas.

plant
A building and the equipment that carry out a process.

sewer
An underground channel that carries drainage water and liquid and solid waste.

tank
A large container for liquids or gas.

water supply
The source, means, or process of supplying water to a community.

Index

To Learn More

FACT SURFER

Finding more information is as easy as 1, 2, 3.

❶ Go to www.factsurfer.com

❷ Enter "wheredoeswatergo" into the search box.

❸ Choose your book to see a list of websites.